How to Build and Improve a Tutoring Practice: A Guide to Mixing Business and Education

by Trevor at JustAddTutor.com

Special offer

This book is not designed to be a summer beach read or a page-turner. Instead, it provides courses of action that you can immediately implement to start a successful new tutoring business, or improve your existing one.

As such, I've designed two <u>free</u> email courses to go along with this book.

The first is a 9 email course called "How to Become a Professional Tutor in 60 Days". You can start the email course at https://gum.co/NbwJ .

The second is a visual guide called "How to Strengthen Your Existing

Tutoring Business". You can download that guide at https://gum.co/MSEB .

Table of Contents

Special offer   1

Introduction   8

How to Craft Your Web Presence as a Tutor   9

The importance of web presence for tutors   9
   Crafting your tutoring web presence   9
      Tutoring credentials   10
      A tutor's practical proof of effectiveness   11
      A tutor's social proof of effectiveness   13
      Tutoring logistics   14
         Location   14
         Schedule   14
         Pricing   14
   The practicalities of actually presenting your tutoring on the web   16
      Letting your friends and acquaintances know that you're a tutor through web presence   16
      Letting everyone else know you're a tutor through web presence   17

	3
Yelp	20
Google My Business	22

How to Craft a Tutoring Website that Makes People Want to Hire You — 23

What to put on your tutoring website — 23

The four factors that make people hire you	23
Information about what tutoring subjects you cover and what you provide	27
Peripheral products	28
Ways to contact you	29
The types of blog posts to write	30
Blog posts that answer questions people ask	31
Blog posts that people will bookmark	32

Marketing Your Tutoring — 33

Marketing techniques that work for tutors

Advertising as a tutor	33
Unsuccessful advertising strategies for tutors	33
Successfully advertising on Google as a tutor	35
Adwords	35
Retargeting ads with Google	36
Always be experimenting with your ads	37
Constructively participating online as a marketing technique	38

	4
Online directories as a tutoring marketing technique	39
SEO for tutors	39
Peripheral products as marketing for tutors	40

Selling Your Services as a Tutor

What a good tutoring client wants — 39

The sales process for tutors — 39

Initial emails for basic information	40
Initial phone call for more in-depth information	42
In-person meeting to seal the deal	43

Practicalities and logistics of tutoring — 48

Setting up web and email hosting for your tutoring	49
Finding a place to do your tutoring	49
Setting prices and getting money for your tutoring services	50
Dress code for tutoring	51
Dealing with difficult clients as a tutor	52
Taxes and deductions for tutoring	52
Bookkeeping	53

How to Teach as a Tutor — 54

Optimal teaching strategy for tutors — 55

General thoughts about teaching	55
Specific recommendations for effective tutoring	56
Create a learning structure	56
Explicit hierarchical structure and progress tracking	56
Goals (short, intermediate, long)	58
Improving the in-class experience	58
Repetition/callback	58
Takeaways from lesson	59
During lessons, vary levels of guidedness	60
Give your students a chance to fail in controlled ways	60
Improvements in Communication	61
Narrative	61
Compliment liberally, criticize gently	61
After Class	62
Supplementary material and long term memory retention	62
Conclusion and Standing Offer	**63**

Introduction

I started trying to support myself solely with independent tutoring a couple years ago, at the beginning of 2016. Before that, I had been working as a tutor and test prep instructor with company in Singapore, and before that I worked as a part-time tutor in college. When I started, I had a fair amount of experience teaching (although it turned out I still had a lot to learn), but I had very little experience running a business.

In 2017, I made almost 6 figures through my tutoring work ($90,189, according to my tax return). In 2018, I'm on track for comfortably over 6 figures. More importantly, I choose my own work schedule, I choose what I want to work on, and my well over 100 clients have been, by and large, delighted to work with me and pay me on my own terms.

Now, I didn't create this book to portray myself as a guru, or to try to pretend that the whole world should become tutors. My income, although comfortable, is not anything compared to a doctor's (as my mom, who is a doctor, likes to remind me). Also, this is far from a get-rich-quick scheme: tutoring is still a job, with cliental expectations and its own forms of drudgery. Lastly, before I was a tutor, I was still academically smart, reasonably social, and a natural teacher. Those were big advantages for me out of the gate, and they won't necessarily be true for everyone.

However, if you are someone like I was, interested in tutoring but having trouble making the leap to a business owner (which is really what you're trying to become), this book is for you. This book presents tutoring as a business, and tells you how to structure that business to achieve success. So, that means you'll learn how to:

1. Design a tutoring website that makes people want to hire you
2. Get potential tutoring clients to look at your website in the first place
3. Convert a tentative email from a potential student into a check
4. Structure your interactions with a student to make them happy to work with you and pay you for a long time
5. Handle paying taxes, getting a website and professional email address, finding a place to work, and all the other annoying practicalities of working on your own.

Essentially, it's a collection of what I've learned to give me the success that I've had. It's what I wish I knew before I started on my journey, and the knowledge that I won through hard work and a lot of failure. I hope you find it worthwhile.

Sincerely,
Trevor Klee

How to Craft Your Web Presence as a Tutor

Executive summary: You need to craft your tutoring web presence to emphasize your credentials, practical proof of your effectiveness, the social proof of your effectiveness, and, to a lesser extent, your pricing, location, and schedule. You do this through LinkedIn, Google My Business, and Yelp.

The importance of web presence for tutors

As an independent tutor, it is almost certain that you will not have your own office. In fact, I'd encourage you not to, because office rent is really expensive, and a slow month is made way more painful by an office lease hanging over your head. I would recommend you get a desk in a coworking space, which costs about $350/month, at least in Boston.

The down side of this is that you are going to miss out on one of the big advantages of having a storefront: visibility. Anybody with a storefront continually broadcasts to the town that they exist. People pass by there every day, and, even if they don't go inside, they know that the store exists. And, if their friends ask them, "Hey, do you know where I could get stationery?", they will have a ready answer, even if they have never bought stationery.

Independent tutors miss out on all of that. Nobody will automatically know that you tutor, or that there is a tutor near them, even if they are in the office next door to you. The only way you can get that visibility is via the Internet.

First, let's discuss what your web presence should entail. Then, we'll discuss the practicalities of actually getting web presence.

Crafting your tutoring web presence

People overcomplicate their web presence. They think they need a clever name, or well-written copy. This is not the case. It is not your job to convince someone that they want a tutor, or that tutoring in general is good. If they're looking for a tutor, they already believe that. Instead, your job is to convince them to hire you.

So, why would anyone hire you as a tutor? Four reasons:

1. Your credentials
2. The practical proof of your effectiveness
3. The social proof of your effectiveness
4. Your logistics (schedule, location, pricing)

When people are choosing to hire a tutor, they are going to consider those four factors. They will not necessarily consider all of them equally (some people are price insensitive, some people don't care about credentials). It is to your advantage, though, to make those four factors as obvious as possible, because people will need to see them before they hire you. If you make it hard to find them (or, even worse, make people ask you for them), you will lose sales to people's natural laziness.

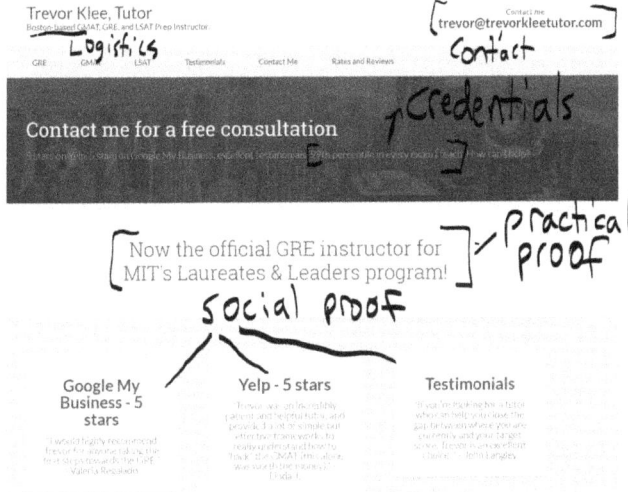

My homepage of my tutoring website: www.trevorkleetutor.com. Notice how prominently the 4 factors are displayed.

Tutoring credentials

A tutor's credentials are not entirely straightforward. There are no governing agencies for tutoring (thank the Lord), and no licensing exams. So, how can you get the little pieces of paper that tell people you're legitimate?

Simple: you make them up. Not that you fake the pieces of paper, but you create their importance. In my case, I emphasize my Ivy League undergraduate education, the academic awards I've won, and the scores I've gotten on standardized tests. This is especially useful for me because I specialize in test prep.

About me

My name is Trevor Klee. I'm a Princeton University graduate with a degree in Geosciences. I've been tutoring for several years now, both in America and abroad in Singapore. I'm currently based in Cambridge, Massachusetts. In my free time, I enjoy Brazilian Jiu Jitsu and creative writing.

Scores

GMAT: 750
GRE: 170V/166Q
SAT: 2350 (800 R/790 W/ 760 M)
ACT: 35

My credentials are standard, good credentials, but they're not the only ones. In the test prep company I used to work for, the website emphasizes the business school the founders went to, the "trademarks" on the teaching method, and the fact that the company experienced mild success in creating their own business school test.

Singapore's Premier Test Prep and Admissions Consultancy

Founded in 2006 by INSEAD alumni, Prep Zone has long been Singapore's largest, most innovative, and most acclaimed test-prep company. The company's **trademarked** teaching methodology, based on unlimited classes and small group sizes, is utilised every year by thousands of students in Singapore. Besides Singapore (our favourite city and HQ), Prep Zone also has teaching centres in India (Mumbai), and in China (Shanghai).

Apart from teaching all major standardised tests, the company also creates and conducts admissions tests for prestigious international schools and universities, such as Euromed, European School of Management and Technology, the Indian School of Business, and INSEAD.

To understand which test score you need or how you should prepare, just give us a ring on 6812-9999 any time. We have a superb international team of consistently-successful teachers, top-scoring test-takers, and recent university graduates, we are passionate enough to work 7 days a week, even on public holidays.

You can copy my made up credentials, my former employer's made-up credentials, or make up your own. You just need some pieces of paper that tell people you're legitimate.

A tutor's practical proof of effectiveness

When I first started, everyone told me that I should have some statistics to tell people. Something like "65% of people who study with me get an 80 point boost". Well, I never developed those statistics, and nobody's ever asked about them.

If people do ask, they normally say something like "Have you ever had a client like me who did well?" Then I tell them stories of clients like them.

So, that exact idea (the statistics idea) isn't really important, even if people tell you it is. But, the idea behind that idea is sound. You need some sort of proof of your effectiveness. Your proof, however, is going to, once again, be made up.

In this case you'll be in good company, to be honest. My mom is a doctor, and she was never asked to produce statistics about the outcomes of her patients. I've never met a lawyer who produces those sorts of statistics either. Instead, what you're going to do for proof is to piggyback off of established institutions or organizations.

In my case, this was quite straightforward. Early on, I was fortunate enough to get a job doing GRE prep at MIT. This gave me money, which was great, because I used it to buy things. But, this also gave me practical proof of my effectiveness. MIT apparently trusted me enough to let me teach their students. Therefore, I implied, other people could trust me to teach their students as well.

Now, my former employer takes a different tact. If we look at their front page again, we'll notice they use newspaper articles they've been mentioned in, their government registration, and schools they've partnered as their practical proof. It's important to note that these "proofs" are made up, in the sense that none of them were awards for how good they are at teaching. The newspaper articles reported on their attempts to create a new business school test, the government registration is a legal formality, and the partnerships are to help the schools find new students in Singapore. But, they could still use these as practical proofs anyways!

Your practical proofs can be anything, really. You likely won't have any when you're just starting out, but you can seek out established institutions or companies to "prove" that you're a qualified tutor.

A tutor's social proof of effectiveness

The Internet age has brought us a great many marvels. One of these marvels is the abundance of social proof that has come with the proliferation of review sites. Simply put, potential clients want to know that other people have worked with you before and liked you. Nobody wants to be your first.

Now, if you play this right, this is actually an advantage of working out of a coworking space vs being in a storefront. In a storefront, traditional social proof was just what people said about a store, or how many people were in the store at any given time. The former was hard for the store to monitor, the latter was hard for the store to control. As an independent tutor, you don't have to play by these rules.

Your social proof is going to come in the form of reviews on Google My Business (the review cards that come up when you Google a store), Yelp, and testimonials. In order to get these reviews, you're first going to need to set your business up on GMB and Yelp (the logistics of which I'll cover later in this blog post), then you're going to need to solicit reviews. I know Yelp says not to solicit reviews, but whatever.

Once you get the reviews, that's your social proof! Don't just leave the reviews on the site, either: take screenshots and post them to your website. Take a look at how I do it.

Reviews

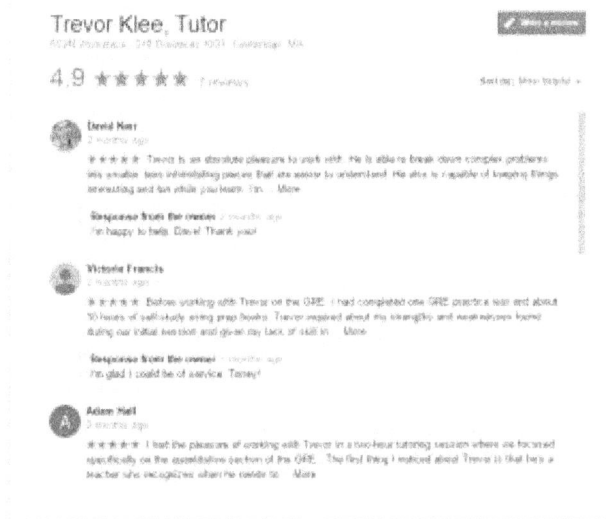

When I first started out, I knew that social proof was incredibly important for me to get. So I actually posted on reddit asking people if I could tutor them for free in exchange for reviews and testimonials. Many people agreed, and then a few actually became my clients afterwards. I've often regarded that as one of the most valuable investments of time I made when I started out.

Tutoring logistics

Logistics are both important and hard to change. We'll cover the important ones in sequence: location, schedule, and pricing.

Location

To be honest, I moved to Boston in part because I thought it'd be a good place to tutor. There are a lot of colleges and graduate schools here, and I thought there'd also be a lot of people looking for tutoring. I was correct. If I had tried to tutor for graduate school exams in Podunk, Michigan, I would have had a tougher time of it.

I also thought a lot about location when I was picking coworking spaces. I've worked in two coworking spaces, and both of them have been very easy to access by public transportation. A lot of people use public transportation in Boston, and if I was working in a place that was hard to get to via public transportation, I'd just be shooting myself in the foot. Also, it'd be annoying for my own commute.

Fortunately, as a tutor, your business is entirely possible to conduct online. In fact, I do conduct a lot of my business online, and for that I just rely on a speedy Internet connection, which I have at home and at work. I video chat over Skype or Google Hangouts, and, when I need to illustrate something, just share my screen and use the OneNote app on my computer (I have a Surface Pro, which lets me draw on it). Before that, I'd just use Google Draw and draw on that while sharing my screen.

You probably can't choose where you live, so my advice would be to pick a location to work that's easy to get to and rely on a speedy Internet connection if they're too far away. Personally, I never travel to clients' locations. That costs money (in terms of car wear and gas), takes a lot of unpaid time, and is generally unpleasant. So, that's another advantage of a nice coworking space: it's a good reason to refuse to travel to people.

Schedule

Being a full time tutor unfortunately means giving up the 9-5. You have to work when people are free, because it's a little too much to ask them to take off work for you every week. I limit my own tutoring schedule to 7 days a week, 10 am to 8 pm. Admittedly, that's not ideal, but that's the way it is.

For you, the worst reason to not get a client is because your schedules just don't match up. So, especially when you start out, be flexible! Work when people want to work with you.

Pricing

Ah, the dreaded topic. It's uncomfortable to bring up and uncomfortable to talk about. So, let's clear the air first. Here's what I charge.

GMAT Tutoring Rates

$1600 for 10 hours
$1100 for 5 hours
$250 for 1 hour

$160/hr for the harder exam

(Note: discounts are available depending on financial need and individual circumstance. Contact me for more information.)

LSAT and GRE Tutoring Rates

$1000 for 10 hours

$625 for 5 hours

$150 for 1 hour

$100/hr

(Note: discounts are available depending on financial need and individual circumstance. Contact me for more information.)

Consulting Rates

$300 for 1 week

$1100 for 1 month

That's way more than what I charged when I first started out. It's a lot of money. And yet, it's still less than, what, say, Manhattan Prep charges.

Flexible Tutoring Packages

25 Hours (includes all books and resources)	$225/hour
20 Hours (includes all books and resources)	$230/hour
15 Hours (includes all books and resources)	$235/hour
10 Hours (includes all books and resources)	$245/hour
5 Hours	$250/hour
Hourly Rate (2 hour minimum)	$255/hour

SIGN UP TODAY

There are two contradictory facts about pricing that we need to consider before we can discuss how much you should charge. The first is that people want to pay less. The second is that people think cheaper things are worse than expensive things. It's your job to find an amount that people are happy paying you and also will respect you for.

To find this, I'd recommend you experiment. I've done a lot of experimenting with my pricing, which is how I've come up with my current prices. If you're looking for a place to start, I'd recommend you charge more than 75% of all prices you see online. That way you're not the most expensive option, but you still clearly position yourself as premium.

On a side note, one thing I've found works for me is allowing people to bargain. First of all, although I'm sure I get paid less than I could, I don't run the risk of losing clients because they're afraid they're getting ripped off. Second of all, I often feel guilty about how much I charge, and this assuages my guilt.

The practicalities of actually presenting your tutoring on the web

When you present your tutoring on the web, you should keep in mind a few things.

First, you need to make sure that your tutoring persona is getting in front of the right people. Almost everyone on the web is not interested in hiring you for tutoring. In fact, it is a statistically insignificant number of people who are interested in hiring you for tutoring. Your goal, then, is to make sure that people who are looking for tutoring are aware of your presence.

Second, you can safely assume that everyone on the Internet generally has a very limited attention span. People can focus on one thing only if it interests them or directly benefits them. Your tutoring presentation is almost certainly not going to be something that interests or benefits them, so present your tutoring in a way that acknowledges their limited attention span. The only exception is when you are writing something about your tutoring that is designed to interest or benefit them. Presenting the reasons they should hire you does not count.

Third and most importantly, when people are looking to hire you, they are probably looking to see your four factors (credentials, practical proof, social proof, logistics), and then they will look to contact you. Make that easy for them! It's lucky that you've been put in front of someone who's looking to hire you. It's highly probable that they are impatient. So make it easy for them to see your factors and to contact you.

The two groups of people who need to be aware of your tutoring business are your friends/acquaintances, and everyone else. So let's cover web presence for those.

Letting your friends and acquaintances know that you're a tutor through web presence

This is easy. First of all, change your job on Facebook. Everyone sees that, and Facebook will notify people that your job title has changed. If you'd like, add a bit of detail about what you specialize in and a link to your website. Then don't do anything more on Facebook, because nobody likes people who spam about their businesses on Facebook.

Second, change your job title on LinkedIn. This is where people actually brag and talk about their career, and it'll also show up high on Google Search results. So, put your 4 factors into play! Give a brief (one paragraph) overview of the subjects you cover, then your credentials, practical proof, social proof, and logistics. If people want to contact you, give them a website link. You can also give them your email, but that will open you up to the spam bots that trawl LinkedIn.

And…that's it for letting your friends and acquaintances know. If your experience is anything like mine, you will not really get much out of your friends and acquaintances. Tutoring is just too rare of a need.

Letting everyone else know you're a tutor through web presence

Okay, so this is the part that actually matters. This works in confluence with your marketing efforts to get people to actually contact you and hire you. If you were a grocery store, your marketing efforts would be the circulars you send around, while your web presence would be your physical storefront.

Of course, you don't actually have a storefront. Instead, you have whatever pops up when people search you or terms related to you. Here's what pops up when I search my name. I have an uncommon name, so, as I'd hope, I dominate the search results.

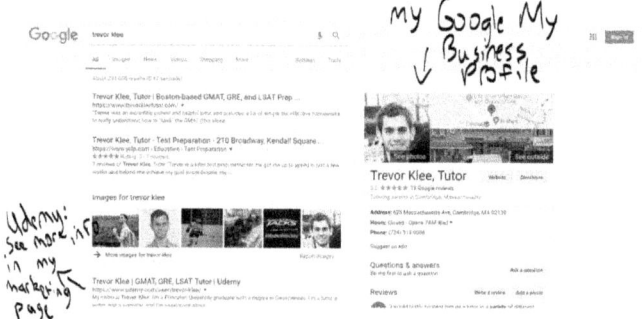

Unfortunately, phrases like "Boston GMAT tutor" are way harder to rank for, even though they're way more valuable (because that's what people search for when they're looking for tutors). Here's my ranking, on the second page of Google search results (where it is highly unlikely people will see it).

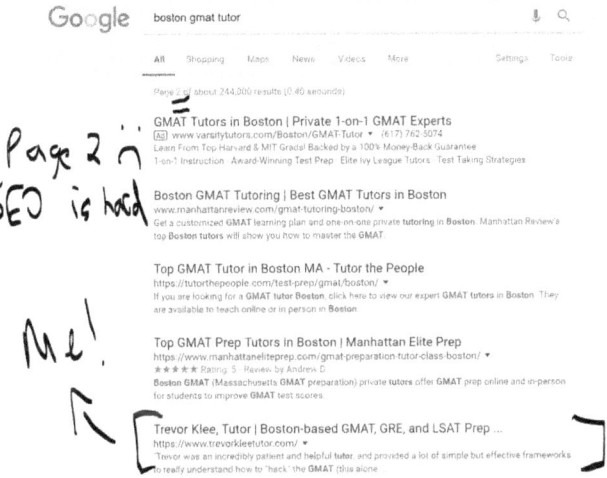

My web presence, then, ends up being a combination of my marketing efforts (as highlighted), my Yelp page (because Yelp is ranked 2nd on "Boston GMAT tutor"), and my Google My Business page. The advantage of the Google My Business page is more obvious when I search "GMAT tutor near me", another common search phrase.

Best Gmat Tutor in Boston, MA

$ $$ $$$ $$$$ ⓘ Open Now   ⇌ All Filters

[Ad] Harvard Student Agencies Tutoring
★★★★☆ 3 reviews
Private Tutors, Tutoring Centers, Test Preparation
🏷 $100 for $125 Deal

Serving Cambridge and the Surrounding Area ⓘ
(857) 529-6356

In advance of our daughter's first (and hopefully final) SAT, we decided on HSA's Customized SAT Prep Package (20 hrs. w/ no online sessions). She worked with three different **tutors**... read more

[Ad] The Princeton Review
Private Tutors, Test Preparation

Serving Newton Center and the Surrounding Area ⓘ
(888) 964-8805

The Princeton Review is a top destination for college- and graduate school-bound students. We offer test preparation and private tutoring for the SAT, ACT, MCAT, GRE, GMAT, LSAT, AP... read more

1. Manhattan Prep
★★★★☆ 14 reviews
Tutoring Centers, Test Preparation, Private Tutors

Serving Boston and the Surrounding Area
(212) 721-7400

5 stars for Manhattan Prep and their great instructor team! I took a course with Sergio Frisoli and found the content and instruction to be incredibly helpful in preparing for the ... read more

2. MyGuru
★★★★★ 3 reviews
Test Preparation, Tutoring Centers, Private Tutors
🏷 $95 for $125 Deal

Serving Boston and the Surrounding Area
(617) 500-4498

On the **tutor** - Priya (recommended by Mark) did an excellent job working with me to refine my quant strategy on the **GMAT** and her efforts, advice and suggestions yielded tangible... read more

Much better on Yelp

3. Trevor Klee, Tutor
★★★★★ 7 reviews
Test Preparation, Private Tutors

Serving Cambridge and the Surrounding Area
(734) 315-0088

I picked Trevor to help me get over the hump on the **GMAT** because of all the great reviews he has. I made the right choice! I had already taken 3 classes and had hit a wall in terms ... read more

27

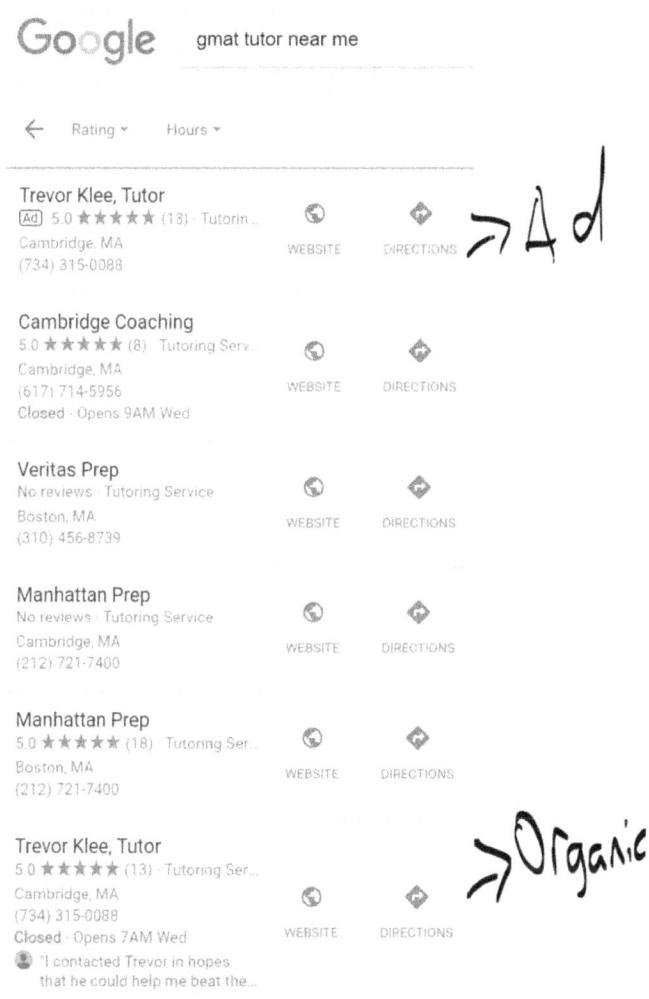

That's my main web presence. Now, there are also other parts, most noticeably my longtail SEO and any tools that I build. These are subjects for a later time.

Yelp

Yelp is critical. A lot of people use Yelp as their first search engine to find local services (like tutors), and it shows up highly on Google search results. Unfortunately, there's not a ton you can do to affect Yelp. Basically, you need to fill out your profile with information, ways to contact you, and nice photos, like my Yelp page from before.

Then, most importantly, you need reviews. According to Yelp, you should never ask any of your clientele for reviews. They have good intentions here, but that's ridiculous, in my opinion. Nobody has ever left me an unsolicited review, because I know each of my clients personally. It's very difficult to leave a review for someone that you have spent a minimum of 10 hours one on one with.

So, if I feel like I've gotten along particularly well with someone, I ask them to leave me a review on Yelp. There is something very important to note here, though. Yelp hides reviews of people who have only 1 review (i.e. of you) or 0 friends. I mean they literally hide them. Look at the screenshot below.

These are actual people who I tutored. They liked my tutoring a lot. They wanted to give me 5 stars. Yelp hid their reviews and they don't affect my rating. Thanks Yelp!

Therefore, when people do agree to leave me reviews, I now explicitly instruct them to review several other places beforehand, wait a couple days, then leave me a review. It's more annoying for my clients, and it's unfortunate, but it's the only way I can guarantee the reviews aren't hidden.

Google My Business

Google My Business is much more straightforward than Yelp once it's set up. You put your pictures, hours, and information up, and then people can leave you reviews. There are no real rules about the reviews people can leave you, either.

However, the tough part is that in order to get a Google My Business account, you need to go through their process and prove that you have a local business. This is a really annoying process. First of all, even though it's supposedly done through an online process, the online process did not work at all. I had to call in to a call center in India. Now, one way of verifying that you're a local business is to take a picture of signage at your address. As a tutor working at a coworking space, I didn't have signage at my address. So, I taped a paper sign to my coworking space, took a picture, and emailed it to them as proof that I was a local business owner.

They didn't want to verify me after that either, so then I just harangued them for a while until they gave up and verified me. I used my secret call center tactic: when they were refusing to help me, I said loudly "This is making me very dissatisfied with your service." When they verified me, I said "I am now very satisfied." Any call center worker who is judged on the degree of satisfaction people have with their call will pay attention to these words. These Google call center workers were no exception. Once the call center worker did what I wanted and heard I was very satisfied, she asked me to fill out a survey at the end so I could rate her highly.

How to Craft a Tutoring Website that Makes People Want to Hire You

Executive summary: In order for people to hire you, they're going to need to see your four factors. If you want to attract people to your website and make it seem more professional, you should also have information about what you cover, what you provide, and any materials you've developed. You should also have a blog that leads people to your website, either through search engines or through helpful posts and tools that people will share. Don't put useless stuff on your blog.

I'm not going to write about the practicalities of putting up a website or finding a template, as I actually have [website templates for sale and download](#) on justaddutor.com, along with instructions for how to put them into effect. The templates I've created follow best practices, and will convert potential tutoring clients into actual tutoring clients better than anything else on the Web. However, what to put on your website is an important subject, so I'm going to discuss that here.

What to put on your tutoring website

Assuming you don't have a physical storefront, your website is the only "place" for your tutoring that you control completely. You can put anything you want on your website, with no limitations. This is a blessing and a curse. If you don't put the right things on your website, it will not convert clients. And, in the end, what you want from your tutoring website is to convert visitors into paying customers.

So, here's what you're going to put on your tutoring website to make sure it converts.

1. The four factors that make people hire you

2. Information about what you cover and what you provide
3. Peripheral products
4. Ways to contact you
5. Blog posts and helpful tools

The four factors that make people hire you

I've already talked extensively about the four factors that make people hire you.
To reiterate, they were

1. Credentials
2. The practical proof of your effectiveness
3. The social proof of your effectiveness
4. Your logistics

Of these, the first 3 should be ubiquitous on your website. The fourth should be clearly available. Let me show you what I mean.

First, I put the first 3 on the front page of my website. I link to the 4th. You should notice that they are all as clear as possible *before the fold* (i.e. before the user has to scroll down to see more). Again, I am always assuming people are lazy. I don't assume they will scroll down.

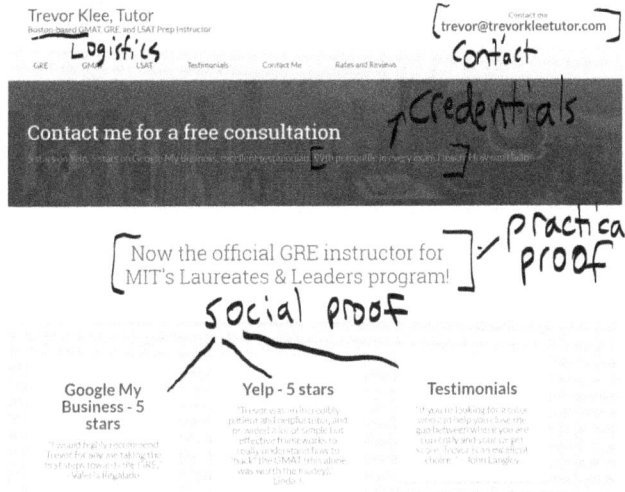

I also put the first 4 on the bottom of every informational page.

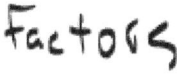

Factors at the bottom of my GMAT informational page. To be honest, I should probably have a contact form here.

I have a separate page for testimonials, for people who are looking for those specifically.

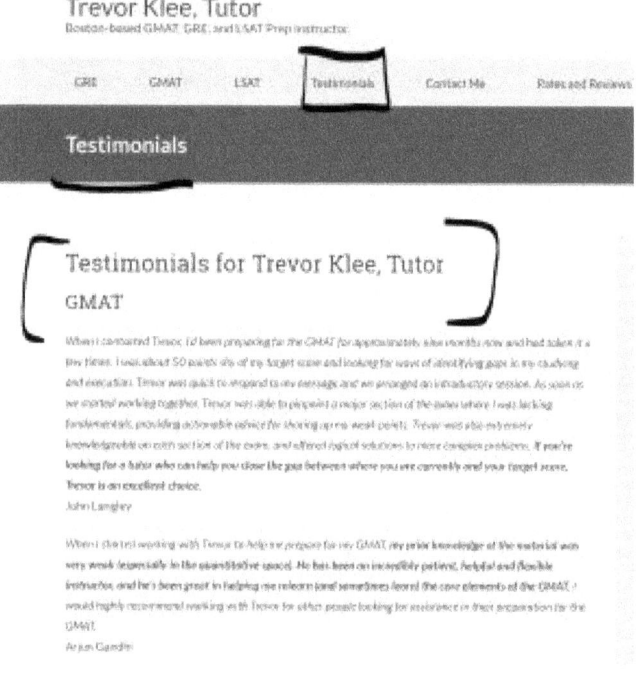

And I put them on my Contact page.

Trevor Klee, Tutor
Boston-based GMAT, GRE, and LSAT Prep Instructor

GRE   GMAT   LSAT   Testimonials   Contact Me   Rates and Reviews

Contact Me

Factors before Contact Form

Welcome!

I provide GMAT and GRE tutoring remotely and in-person. I have a 98th percentile score on the GMAT, 95th percentile scores on the GRE, and I'm the official GRE instructor for MIT. More importantly, I have a 5 star rating on Google My Business and a 5 star rating on Yelp for my tutoring.

Please fill out the form below for a free consultation.

Contact Me

Fill out the form below for a free consultation about studying for the GRE or GMAT.

Name:

Lastly, I put them before my rates, so people have to look at them before they can look at my rates.

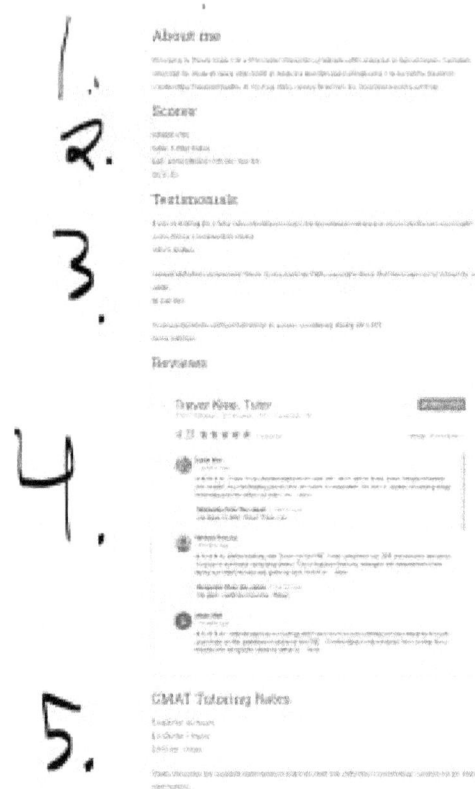

I make people look through all of my factors before they get to see my pricing. My pricing is very justified.

Is it redundant? Yes. But people don't read a tutoring website like they read an informational website (like the one you're reading now). They're (hopefully) reading your tutoring website because they're looking to hire you. If they get the right vibes, they will stop reading your website and contact you. That's what you want.

So make sure they get the right vibes to contact you, wherever they happen to be looking on your website. Then make sure they can contact you.

Information about what tutoring subjects you cover and what you provide

Any sales pitch you make will be stronger if you're a specialist, regardless of your credentials. This should be pretty obvious. After all, if you had the choice of getting a root canal from a Nobel Prize winner or a dentist, you'd pick the dentist every time. The Nobel Prize winner is smart, but you'd rather just have someone who knows how to do a root canal.

One of the purposes of your website is to tell people what you provide, and show people that you have competence. Now, *the most common mistake I see people make when they tutor is that they list 20,000 subjects, and claim to be experts in all of them.* Don't do that! Nobody will trust you over a specialist.

Instead, what you need to do is to specialize. Pick your subjects (I picked 3 major tests), and, on your website, list out your conception of the subject and your approach to them. It does not have to be brilliant, you just have to show that you've thought a lot about these subjects and how to teach them.

Take a look at how I approach the GMAT. I probably provide less information than I should, but at least I show clearly that I'm knowledgeable about the GMAT and I have a standardized approach to teaching it.

The Graduate Management Admission Test (GMAT) is a required test for most graduate management programs. It's delivered in English on computer, and measures Analytical Writing, Verbal, Quantitative, and Integrated Reasoning skills. Of these skills, by far the most important are the verbal and quantitative sections, which measure your logical, grammatical, mathematical, and math reasoning abilities.

My teaching style

Most test preparation companies try to convince you that the GMAT is impossibly difficult, and it is only with their help that you might possibly survive it. I don't believe this. The GMAT is hard, but it's not impossible. It's irresponsible of an educator to intimidate their students, and so I do the opposite.

My teaching style strives to make the GMAT seem conquerable. I provide a clear roadmap to success, easy-to-understand techniques and strategies to get there, and continual encouragement and support to my students. My goal is solely to make my students succeed on the GMAT with a minimum amount of stress on their part. That's it.

What comes with a tutoring package

1. An easy to follow, thorough study plan
2. My comprehensive GMAT guide: The Clear, Simple Guide to the GMAT
3. Unlimited email support
4. Structured, helpful tutoring sessions

About me

My name is Trevor Klee. After graduating from Princeton, I worked as a tutor in Singapore, tutoring undergraduate and graduate exams. While there, I learned the ins and outs of the GMAT, eventually getting myself to a 750. From there I moved to Boston, and decided to dedicate myself to Boston GMAT prep, as well as to other graduate level exams.

Sample review

Bryan Um
2 months ago

★★★★★ Trevor has the unique ability to break down a complicated question into a few simple steps so that I could replicate the same process with other problems. I would definitely recommend him as a GMAT tutor for anyone who needs an extra boost in his/hers/their final score.

Information about the GMAT, my approach to it, and what comes with my tutoring. Not super in-depth, but enough to show that I've thought about it.

Anyone who looks at that page is going to be convinced that, if they want to know about the GMAT, I'm someone they should talk to. Indeed, sometimes people do just want to talk to me about the uses of the GMAT, or the GMAT vs the GRE, or even how to get into business school. This is because I've convinced them I have a lot of domain-area expertise.

In this sense, your messaging strategy is going to come hand-in-hand with your business strategy. As a tutor, I'd advise you to pick things to specialize with and stick with them. This is going to give you a deeper understanding not just of the subject, but of the ways that other people think of the subject. You are going to be better at teaching the subject than someone who has not spent the time working with it and with students of it that you have.

In the same vein, you need to communicate through your website that you have thought a lot about the specific subject the student is interested in learning. This is, in the end, the point of putting information about the subject on your website. You're not looking to actually inform the student, but you are looking to tell them that you know a lot about teaching the subject.

Peripheral products

As I've mentioned, I think peripheral products are a fantastic idea for any tutor. Now, I prefer to sell my tutoring products through Gumroad. I advertise them through Google and Reddit. But, I also have links to them on my website.

LSAT videos. I'm currently experimenting with the best way to sell them, which is why the format is wonky. I'll report back once I have answers.

My reasoning is simple. I've spent a lot of money and effort getting people to my website. If I can make some money by selling them products while they're there, I'll be happy.
Also, it adds to my credibility.

Ways to contact you

As I've said repeatedly, one of my cardinal rules on the Internet is that people are lazy. If it is not obvious how to contact you, people will not contact you. (Also, to be honest, people tend to be sort of dumb, too. Sometimes when it is obvious how to contact you, people still won't figure out how to contact you.)

Your website needs to make it obvious how to contact you. For me, I just put a "Contact Us" page and my email in the top right of my website.

I have relatively few ways of contacting me because I work primarily with technologically savvy young adults who are comfortable using contact forms and emails. If, on the other hand, you are working with an older crowd (like if you're tutoring teenagers and will be hired by their parents), I'd highly encourage you to make it even easier to contact you. First of all, get a floating "Contact Us" form. Second of all, put your phone number on your website as well.

Don't worry, you don't need to put your cell phone on your website. You can get a free Google Voice number, which comes with a free mailbox and text messaging service. Still, it is safe to assume that anyone over the age of 35 prefers to call when it's an important matter, like hiring an expensive tutor for their child. You should make it easy for them to get you on the phone, or at least leave a voicemail.

The types of blog posts to write

Blog posts and helpful tools are going to be a critical part of your web presence. If you write helpful blog posts and make useful tools, people will find your website. Then they might buy your peripheral products or hire you as a tutor.

For example, one blog post I wrote regularly brings people to my website who are wondering about the accuracy of practice tests designed by various companies.

158 views per month from people who just find this page through Google. Pretty good investment, especially considering these are 158 GMAT and GRE takers.

Meanwhile, a tool I created ranks highly on Google on the forum I posted it on. This tool links directly back to my website, and brings visitors there.

Second to last on the first page of Google. It's not where I want it to be, but it's only been up for a month.

So, writing blog posts and creating tools is important. But, there's a caveat here. Most advice to online businesses just stops there and says "now go create some stuff!"

That's not a good idea. Don't create blog posts for the sake of creating blog posts. You're going to clutter up your website and tire yourself out. There are really only two sorts of blog posts you should be creating.

1. Blog posts that answer questions people ask

2. Blog posts that are useful enough to bookmark (this includes tool announcements)

That's it. No "5 Reasons Why Studying for the SAT Is Fun!", or recapitulated news articles. Huffington Post can get away with that because they don't pay their contributors. If you value your time, stick to the 2 I mentioned.

Blog posts that answer questions people ask

People ask Google a lot of questions. If you answer those questions, there's a fair chance Google will pick up your blog post and display it in search results. This is good!

There are a few ways to think about what questions to answer in your blog posts. One of them is to just answer the questions that you commonly hear from clients, or that you yourself had during the studying process. If there was some point of test registration that was unclear, or a textbook with a strange explanation, and you had a question about it, probably a lot of other people do too.

Another is to use Google keyword planner to find good topics. From there, you can type the topic into Google and see what comes up in autocomplete. For example, try typing in "does the GMAT" into Google.

What does it autosuggest? Do you have any good answers?

I would warn you, though. Make sure you check out the currently existing answers. You need to create something that's better than what's out there, or at least different.

Blog posts that people will bookmark

Your other option is to create blog posts that people will bookmark. These are posts that you spent a lot of time on in order to develop something useful. How-to guides, collections of links, or organizational tools all qualify.

The one thing to be cautious of here is that these posts are not designed to be picked up by Google. Even if you spent a lot of time on these, nobody will see them if you don't spread them around.

So, my advice would be to post them on relevant subreddits, forums, and blog sites (like Medium). It would be a terrible shame for these posts just to go to waste.

Marketing Your Tutoring

Executive Summary: Successfully marketing as an independent tutor means marketing your website over the Internet. You can use paid Internet marketing through Google, or free Internet marketing techniques like SEO and constructive online participation. Whatever you do, experiment with it constantly. You will not get your marketing strategy right the first time around.

I have tried (and continue to try) many different marketing techniques. Most of them did not work. This chapter is about marketing techniques that did work for me.

As should be obvious, this is based on my experience in my niche (graduate exam test prep). I can't say that this is true for everyone at every time. As I've mentioned before, if you ever want to test a marketing technique, I'd recommend you use the [Traction framework](). It's not brilliant, but it is a good way to think about marketing as experimentation (rather than art).

Without any further ado, the marketing techniques that worked for me as a tutor were:

1. Google advertising
2. Constructively participating in online communities with clear links back to my website
3. Online directories
4. Search engine optimization
5. Selling peripheral products

Let me elaborate on those below.

Marketing techniques that work for tutors
Advertising as a tutor

I have tried a lot of different forms of paid advertising. I've tried print, sandwich-boards (seriously), flyers, and on various websites. The only one that's been really successful has been Google, and it's the only one I still use. Let me run through the rest of these quickly, then I'll explain how I use Google ads.

Unsuccessful advertising strategies for tutors

Print
I advertised both in my parents' temple newsletter and in Harvard College's newspapers. I didn't get any results whatsoever. Quite frankly, I'm not sure who reads them. I got the sense that I could have advertised a free Lamborghini and would have had no leads.

Flyers
Hundreds of flyers got me one lead, and he gave up before we started working together.

Yelp ads (not just the free posting)
Advertising with Yelp is strange. The first month I advertised with Yelp, I immediately got two really solid leads. I was delighted. Then, I advertised with Yelp for several more months, and got nothing. I looked it up online, and a lot of people have had a similar experience. Yelp is great when you try it at first, and then is terrible afterwards. I guess they only have a limited number of leads to go around, and dole them out disproportionately to new advertisers.

I gave up on Yelp after this experience. I still invested in reviews on Yelp, but I didn't give them any more money. I have no regrets about this, especially as the minimum package is $300/month.

Also, be aware that Yelp has very pushy salespeople. They will call you up repeatedly and ask you for ads. Reports online say that if you are mean to them, they will demote your page. There have been lawsuits about it. So, once you decide not to advertise with Yelp, be very polite to their salespeople anyways. I usually tell them I've run out of budget.

Facebook ads
Ach, screw Facebook ads. They're the worst. Basically, Facebook promises that you can use their advertising to pinpoint exactly the consumer that you want to advertise to. Do you sell penguin washing machines? You can advertise to dirty penguin owners in your area!

Unfortunately, the reality is much worse. You see, there are a lot of people who lie on Facebook about who they are and what they do. These are mostly bored, unemployed people. These are also the people who click on your Facebook ads, because they're really bored and want to see what's going on. Facebook, in its infinite wisdom, decides that your business, whatever it is, must therefore really want to appeal to bored, unemployed people, regardless of who you actually want to target.

Long story short, I wasted hundreds of dollars on Facebook before I tracked down the fact that everyone who clicked on my ads was bored, unemployed, and had lied about being in my target demographic. The only Facebook ads that even vaguely worked were when I just treated it like a billboard: location only, no demographics at all.

Don't advertise with Facebook.

LinkedIn ads
Same problem as Facebook. I thought I was advertising to people in my target demographic. Then I'd look at who actually clicked on my ads, and they were way, way out of my target demographic.

Bing
Nobody uses Bing. You're welcome to try it, as Bing is pay per click, but you're not going to have success.

Reddit
Reddit is actually alright to advertise on, but I couldn't get enough out of it for the time I was putting into it. The plus side is that I could carefully target my ads to specific communities, and ads were pretty cheap. The downside is that there's so, so much adblocking on Reddit. The communities I was advertising to are

technologically adept and rather small (only like 5000 registered), so if a significant proportion block my ads, there really just weren't enough people to make it worth my time.

I'd recommend you experiment with Reddit. If there are enough people in your target community, and not too many adblock, you might find that it's worth your efforts.

Successfully advertising on Google as a tutor

Google, in contrast to what I discussed above, is actually great for advertising as a tutor. It is the only advertising service I use now. I spend between $100 and $200 a month there, and it's a major source of my clients.

I use a combination of Adwords and retargeting. Let me explain how they work.

Adwords

Adwords are the ads that appear when people search. These ads are fantastic, because you are reaching people literally when they are searching for it. It's like if someone said at a party, "Oh hey, do you know the best widget spinner?" And then you burst through the wall like the Kool Aid man and say, "I'm an awesome widget spinner! Talk to me!"

Your Adwords should come in two flavors.

a) Adwords direct ads

These are the ads that you buy for keywords like "best math tutor in New York" or "SAT prep company". Basically, it's when people are searching to buy your exact services. This is obviously really, really valuable, and these ads will be very expensive per click (all AdWords are per click). Do not waste clicks, or you will waste a lot of money.

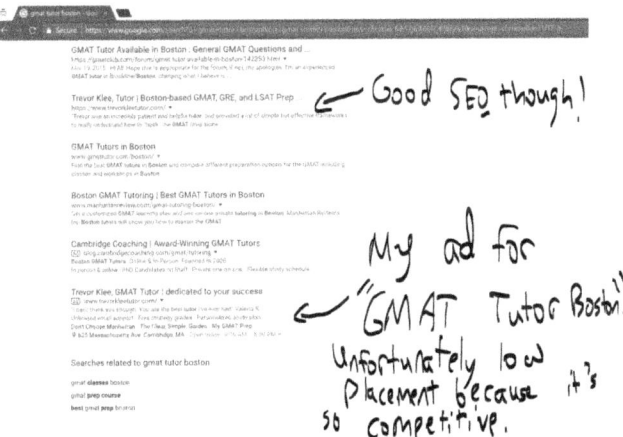

You should be aware with these ads that Google tries to set up their ads to cost you as much money as possible. You need to go into the advanced settings and limit the location and keywords that your ads are set to. Google will encourage users in Timbuktu to click on your ads, but you do not want that (unless you're located in Timbuktu). They will also encourage people searching "best free business consultants" to click on your ad, and you do not want that either.

b) Adwords long tail ads

These are the other sort of ads that you should buy. They're cheap because they're not obviously denoting direct interest. For instance, you might buy ads for searches for your competitor's name, or ads for a complementary product's name. Those are the easiest, then you have to get more creative for other long tail ads. If you want inspiration, use the Google keyword planner. Search some terms related to your business and see what comes up around them.

For my Competitor's name.

> Manhattan Prep GMAT classes | not a smart move
> [Ad] www.trevorkleetutor.com
> Manhattan Prep GMAT classes waste your time and money. There's a better way.

Landing page is really important for these, as is copy. People will not expect you to sell your services on these searches, and they'll be put off by it even if they click on your ad. Make sure you immediately explain how your page relates to their search, then your credentials, social proof, and an obvious means of contacting you. Once again, assume they're impatient, but also assume they're super confused as to why they're being sold your services.

Retargeting ads with Google

Retargeting ads are so awesome. Basically, retargeting means that when people land on your website, Google notices that they landed on your website. Then your ads will follow them around the Internet no matter where they go. Amazon uses them all the time, if you've noticed ads for products you've looked at following you around the Internet.

They're really cool because people will often look at your page when they're weighing their options. This is a reminder of you as an option. Like, imagine if you were shopping for prom dresses, and you tried on 20. But the store clerk, for some reason, repeatedly reminded you of how pretty the backless dress in green was, as you were trying on all the different prom dresses. You'd buy the backless dress in green, right?

And retargeting ads are super cheap. They're display ads (so mostly pictures, and not words), and you're only bidding against yourself, so you will pay nothing for highly targeted ads. As I'll talk about, this is also a huge incentive to get people to go to your website by any means necessary, because then you can sell them super cheap ads.

Unfortunately, it's a total pain [to set up Google retargeting](). It took me forever, because Google has rules about how many people need to go to your website before they'll allow you to retarget them. Just be patient while working through the process of setting up the ads, because they are 1000% worth it.

Always be experimenting with your ads

I put this as a separate point because I think it's really, really important. For both types of AdWords and for retargeting, you should always, always be experimenting with your ads. Change the wording, the images, and the landing pages. You will not get it right the first time. You need to figure out the most effective wording and images to get people to click on the ads, then the most effective landing pages to contact you.

It's really easy to set up A/B experiments. First, find two (or three) configurations of wording that you like. Test them all out and see which gets the highest click through. Then, once you get the best there, find two or three configurations of landing pages that you like. Test them out and see what gets the highest contact rate (which you can figure out based on how many people click through).
Lather, rinse, repeat. Always be experimenting. If you don't, you will waste money, and you won't get the customer leads that you need.

☐ ● Ad

☐ ○ 170/166 GRE Tutor
www.trevorkleetutor.com
Get tutoring from a 99th percentile
GRE tutor. Free 1st lesson!

☐ ○ 700+ GMAT Score
www.trevorkleetutor.com
Get a 700+ GMAT score with a 99th
percentile tutor. Free 1st lesson!

☐ ○ 99th Percentile GRE Tutor
Get The Score You Need
www.trevorkleetutor.com
Get tutoring from MIT's official GRE tutor
Better GRE score guaranteed

☐ ○ 99th percentile GRE Tutor
www.trevorkleetutor.com
Get tutoring from MIT's official
GRE tutor. Free consultation!

☐ ● 99th Percentile GRE Tutor
MIT's GRE Instructor
www.trevorkleetutor.com
"You are the best teacher I've ever had" -
Valerie R. Free consultation

☐ ○ 99th Percentile GRE Tutor
MIT's GRE Instructor
www.trevorkleetutor.com
"You are the best teacher I've ever had" -
Valerie R. Free consultation

☐ ○ Boston GMAT Tutor
www.trevorkleetutor.com
750 GMAT score by MIT's official
GRE instructor. Free consultation!

Each one of these is an ad variation that I've tested. This is only a fraction of all the ones I've tested. Seriously: always experiment!

Constructively participating online as a marketing technique

People discuss everything online over a variety of mediums. This should be obvious. One excellent way of getting clients is to participate in discussions, especially if you tutor online and aren't limited to clients in your geographic location.

The forums I've participated in are primarily Reddit, GMATClub, and GREClub. The latter two are forums specific to the tests I specialize in. You'll probably find similar to whatever you specialize in (if you don't, create them!)

When you participate, it's important to be constructive. Your goal is to portray yourself as someone knowledgeable, trustworthy, and able to help your tutoring client reach their goals. If people post looking for help, comment with something that helps them. Don't sell your services in places where they're unwanted or unexpected!

Instead, if you are helpful on the Internet, and clear about the fact that you are a tutor (hint: your username should have the word "tutor" in it), people will seek you out for themselves. If they don't, you can still use online communities to your advantage. Here's how:

Roughly 75% of your participation should be purely constructive commentary, with no commercial links. With the other 25%, you can

1. Post blog posts that you've written. Your blog posts are on your website, which has clear links to contact you for your services, and has retargeting pixels to advertise to people who've visited you.

2. Festoon your profile with links to your website and descriptions of your services. If it's a forum, you can do the same thing with your signature.

3. Post tools you've created that link back to your services. I'm a big fan of creating well-constructed Google Sheets that help people self-study. These Sheets contain links to my website.

4. Offer free (or free-ish) content or services.

    This is purely an upsell: if people like your free stuff, they might pay you as well. For instance, I offered very cheap LSAT livestreams on Reddit.

In the end, you want to be seen as a valued member of the online community who also sells tutoring services. If people dislike you, or if people don't know you tutor, you've wasted your time.

Online directories as a tutoring marketing technique

There are a lot of online directories. The ones that every tutor has to be on are Yelp and Google My Business, which I discussed in "Web Presence". However, there are others which can work as well. [UniversityTutor](#) has sent a few clients my way, which was well worth the half-hour I spent setting myself up there. Other, city-specific directories might be useful as well.

Out of principle, I refuse to participate in directories that don't let me link out to my own website, or use my own full name. Wyzant and Varsity Tutors are both predatory organizations which simply use their dark arts of SEO to squat at the top of Google's rankings and hoover up leads. Both of them will take a huge amount of your earnings. I got into tutoring to avoid this sort of behavior from an in-person boss. I'm not going to accept it from some unethical startup.

SEO for tutors

Search Engine Optimization is important for tutors because that's the most common way people find a tutor. They search for it on Google.

Now, SEO is something that most people regard as black magic, but is actually super straightforward. Google wants to find websites that people want to read. That's its business. If you create a website that's clearly laid out (using HTML standards like headers and paragraphs), containing information that people search for, Google will find your website and show it to people when they search. If it doesn't find your website, you can [submit it](#).

This should already be covered in [the blog posts you've written](#). However, the other thing I'd say is quality links from other websites are the most important thing for SEO.

This is frustrating, because it can seem a lot like a Catch-22. You need authority to get backlinks (because who's going to link to a nobody?), but you can't get authority without backlinks. This is when networking can come into play. Links from non-profits, established businesses, and established tutors or consultants can all help with SEO. The best way to get these links is to ask.

Peripheral products as marketing for tutors

Developing and selling peripheral products are a great way of getting people to your website. I've developed and sold books, live video courses, and email courses. I wrote the books and the content for the email courses on Google Drive and recorded the videos on Youtube. Then, I sold them all through Gumroad.

Gumroad is a platform which makes it super convenient to sell your own content. They charge you a flat fee of $10/month to sell stuff on there, and you end up getting a solid, professional looking sales flow. I embed the Gumroad links right on my website (which is a straightforward process), and this allows me to retarget everyone who comes to buy content from my website.

Books are easiest to sell, because you just upload the pdf and people can buy it as they please. You can either set it as a flat fee, or as a "pay-what-you-want" with minimums. I do the latter, because people can be surprisingly generous. One of my books is offered for

$1, and I regularly get people voluntarily paying $5 or $10 for it.

I sold videos by uploading the videos on Youtube privately, so there was no way of finding the videos by searching. Then, I sold pdfs with the links to the Youtube videos in the pdf. Email courses were also sold as pdfs, except anyone who bought that specific pdf got a pre-programmed series of emails that followed. I marketed that course as a "Achieve Your Goal in 3 Months" sort of deal.

I market these peripheral products in the same way as I market myself: my credentials, proof of the products, social proof of the products. In this case, I put everything necessary on the cover of the book, because people judge books by their covers. Credentials, social proof (testimonials from initial users), and proof are all right there to be judged.

On a side note, Gumroad collects the email addresses of everyone who buys your products, and gives you a lot of tools to market to them. I'd say about 15% of people give me one time email addresses (so you can't send them another message), and 85% of people give me their legitimate email addresses.

You should experiment with email marketing. I hear great things. Unfortunately, I really haven't, so… I can't say much more. Hey, I can't do everything, right?

Selling Your Services as a Tutor

Executive Summary:

1. Start with a short email chain to find out about their situation. End by scheduling a phone call. This should be 3-4 emails long.

2. Have a phone call where you find out even more about their situation. End by scheduling an in-person (or over videochat) meeting. This phone call should be 10-15 minutes.

3. Have an in-person (or over video chat) meeting where you explain your tutoring strategy, how it applies to them, and the logistics of tutoring. End by confirming pricing and the first tutoring session. This meeting should be 20-30 minutes.

Tutoring is an inbound sales gig. By this, I mean that leads contact you through email or phone by virtue of your marketing efforts. You do not cold call or cold email leads in order to to get them to work with you, for the most part. This is a good thing, too, as cold calling is nerve-wracking and unpleasant.

The sales process I use for my tutoring is designed to efficiently get people from that initial contact to paying me, without making it seem like that's what I'm trying to do. After all, although you're trying to get paid, your client is trying to learn. They're not averse to paying you, but they want to make sure they're getting bang for their buck.

In fact, now is probably a good time to discuss what it is a potential good client wants. I'm specifying "good", here, because you will occasionally get jerks who contact you who want to act like jerks. Those people you will likely not want to work with, unless you need the money enough to put up with their nonsense.

What a good tutoring client wants

A good client wants to hire someone who they are confident can and will work with them to achieve their goals. They understand that it is ultimately their own responsibility to achieve their goals, but they need someone to teach them how and to motivate them. As such, they are looking for someone knowledgeable, reliable, and confidence-boosting. Once they find a person like that, they are willing to pay them a fair rate for their expertise.

Given that's what a good tutoring client wants, the sales process of a tutor is to convince a client that you are knowledgeable, reliable, and confidence-boosting. You want to convince the client that, if they work hard, you can help them achieve their goals. Then, once they're convinced of your worth, you ask for a money and time commitment.

Fortunately, because this is an inbound sales process, a lot of the work is already done for you by your marketing efforts. You don't have to go above and beyond to convince the client. They contacted you because they were already somewhat convinced by the work you put in. You just need to seal the deal. Here's how you do so.

The Sales Process for Tutors

I developed my sales process over a lot of experimentation. This was painful experimentation, because when I got it wrong I would lose a potential client. By opportunity cost, it probably cost me around $20,000 to develop this process. So, pay attention, because this is some expensive information.

My sales process is as follows:

1. Initial emails to get basic information about them (2-3 short emails sent by me)
2. Phone call to get more in-depth information about them, and answer any immediate questions they have (10-15 minutes on the phone)
3. In person meeting or video chat to explain what they can expect from working with me, as well as to arrange pricing and logistics (20-30 minutes in-person or over video chat)

Initial emails for basic information

When people first contact me, they usually send me something like the following message.

```
                    ....edu via papa.iwebfusion.net
   to trevor

       ▓▓▓▓▓ sent you a message from IP: ▓▓▓▓▓
   | Name:    | ▓▓▓▓▓▓▓                                           |
   | E-mail:  | ▓▓▓▓▓▓▓▓▓▓                                        |
   | Phone:   | ▓▓▓▓▓▓▓                                           |
   | Subject: | GMAT Consultation                                 |
   | Details: | Hi Trevor,                                        |
   |          |                                                   |
   |          | I'm looking for a tutor so I can start to prepare to retake the GMAT |
   |          | the first week of June. I'm focused mainly on improving my |
   |          | quantitative score and as you can see I don't have a lot of |
   |          | time                                              |
```

It's a short, concise message, written by someone who needs a tutor for a specific reason. As such, they are almost certainly going to be a good client for me. However, I am not going to jump into calling them, or immediately asking them for payment, or anything like that. I want to sell my services to her, but I don't want her to feel like she's being "sold".

Instead, I respond with a short message, so she knows I've seen her email and I'm interested in her personally. One of the big advantages of being a one-man shop is that I can be personal, and I take advantage of that with my sales process.

I send another follow up email to her for a bit more information. Then I ask for a time to talk to her on the phone.

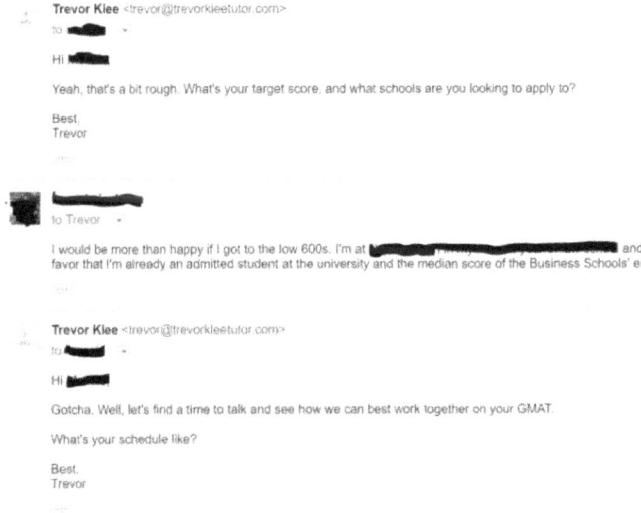

And that's it for the initial emails. We scheduled a time to talk over the phone, and now we're set.

You see? It's not rocket science, or some incredibly slick, sneaky sales process. This woman already knew that I was a good tutor because she had seen my website. She just needed to be reassured that I cared about her individual situation, which any tutor has to do. Once we covered that, we could arrange for the initial phone call.

Initial phone call for more in-depth information

Once I schedule the phone call, I call them (or they call me) at the appointed time. I am always incredibly punctual for anything having to do with tutoring, and this is no exception. If people are paying you per hour, they want you to show up on time.

The importance of punctuality should be obvious, but I'm always amazed when I try to hire someone and they can't show up for our first meeting on time. The most important and basic part of selling is that you promise something, then they pay you for it. In the case of tutoring, you promise that you can help them academically. If they can't trust your promises, they will not pay you for your promises. Therefore, the first thing that you promise them (a phone call at a certain time), needs to be a promise you keep unless you absolutely have to postpone.

Anyhow, I usually start off the phone call by introducing myself (if I called them). I make a little bit of small talk: "How are you?" "Weather's nice now, isn't it?" "You're in the Seaport District, right?"

Then, I segue into talking about tutoring in a pretty blunt fashion. I just say, "So, you're interested in tutoring for the GMAT, right?" Often, they'll say yes, and just start talking on their own. If they start talking on their own, great! *This initial phone call should feature them talking as much as possible.* I just continue to ask open-ended questions about them, their studying, and their tutoring as they talk.

If they don't start talking on their own, first I start by confirming the information we already covered in the emails. Then, I go on to ask them questions about their tutoring goals, educational background, and relevant information to our working together: what's their weekly schedule like (i.e. do they have time to study)? What's their timeline like for completing the exam? Do they have test anxiety? What are their goal scores?

These are pretty similar questions to what I asked over email, and serve much the same purpose. It makes them feel confident that I care about them and their individual circumstance.

If they have any direct questions for me, I will answer them on the call. Some people don't have any questions, and I'm okay with that. Other people have questions that they absolutely want to get answered on our first phone call, and I'm okay with that too.

Once the conversation hits a natural lull, I say, "Well, for next steps, let's find a time to talk in person at my office. I can answer any lingering questions you might have, and go over my tutoring philosophy. After that meeting, if everything is good, we can find a time to start work together."

I arrange a specific time and place for our in-person meeting while we're still on the phone, then I hang up. Then, I immediately confirm our meeting time and place over email.

Don't let them hang up the phone without confirming a meeting time! If you don't confirm an in-person meeting time, the ball is in their court. And, if the ball is in the client's court, it will be a long time (if ever) that you hear from them again.

In-person meeting to seal the deal

Once again, I'm punctual at my in-person meeting. When I meet them, I greet them and make a bit of small talk. I ask them if they want any coffee, water, or tea. Then I lead them to where we're meeting, which is preferably the same quiet conference room I have my tutoring sessions in.

First, I ask them if they have any lingering questions I can answer. These I answer immediately and directly. After that, I launch into my tutoring philosophy spiel.

In my spiel, I explain how I use a practice test to gauge a student's initial strengths and weaknesses. From there, I develop an initial lesson plan to fix their weaknesses and shore up their strengths. Once we both feel that the initial problems have been addressed, the student takes another practice test and we reiterate.

I also explain the error log, which is a subject for another blog post. I explain how I've found that error logs are very effective tools because they force students to focus on what they're weak on (which is a hard thing to force yourself to do), and, through periodic review, allows them to capture the breadth of the broad exams that I teach. They also serve as a visual record of everything the students have learned, which is a nice motivation.

The disadvantage of the error log, I explain, is that focusing on things you're bad at and redoing them if you get them wrong is not fun. Test preparation, I tell them, sucks. However, because I want them to work on their own time as well as with me, I will allow and encourage them to email me whenever they have questions about the subject we're learning.

The point of this spiel is explain what to expect from tutoring to clients, to reassure them that I have a plan, and to gently let them know that the onus of improving is on them. Also, I can tell them that I will support them in achieving their goals, even beyond our immediate meetings.

I ask them if everything I said makes sense. That's their chance to ask questions. If they don't, then I move the subject to pricing.

What I say is: "Normally I charge $160/hr for GMAT tutoring, and I ask for a minimum of 10 hours. Given your current score and your goal, I don't think we'll have any trouble hitting that minimum. But is that price okay with you?"

If they say no, or seem hesitant, I say: "I also offer discounts to people depending on their individual circumstance. For people I discount tutoring for, I normally charge them around $130 to $140 per hour."

Then we decide on an hourly rate. I inform them that I accept Venmo and Paypal, and ask which one they use. Then I tell them that I'll need them to pay for 5 hours or 10 hours of tutoring in advance.

Finally, we once again set up a time to meet, this time for our first tutoring session. I make sure they know that we're meeting for 2 hours for our first meeting, and that I'll need them to send me money and complete a practice test beforehand.

Then we're done! I immediately send them an email after they leave confirming our meeting time. I also ask for 5 or 10 hours payment, and give them information on how to pay me. And I send them a practice test, and ask them to complete it before we meet.

Practicalities and logistics of tutoring

The practicalities of tutoring are intimidating when you're first starting out, and then pretty straightforward afterwards. Here's a list of what I'm going to cover.

1. Setting up web and email hosting
2. Finding a place to work
3. Setting prices and getting money for your services
4. Dress code
5. Dealing with difficult clients (no shows, lateness, and cancellation fees)
6. Taxes and deductions
7. Bookkeeping

NOTE: If you're on Kindle, these links are mostly affiliate links, so I get paid if people sign up through them. However, rest assured that I do not link out to any service I do not personally like and recommend. Also, if you do sign up through these links, thanks! Don't worry, you won't pay more than if you signed up normally.

Setting up web and email hosting for your tutoring

When you get started with a traditional company, you need real estate and a mailbox. When you get started with an online tutoring business, you need virtual real estate and a virtual mailbox. These come in the form of web hosting and email. You can think of your website as the store you build on top of your real estate.

For web and email hosting, I use IWebFusion. They're a small company and their prices are pretty cheap. The upside of their being small is that they are nice and have good customer service. The downside is that they don't have the processes in place of a larger company, so you will need to do more on your own.

If you're unfamiliar with web and email hosting, and want an easy way to set it up, go with Dreamhost. They're a larger company with set processes in place for everything you want to do. They are more expensive (like $40 more per year), so it depends on what you want.

For your website (the "building" on top of your virtual real estate), you should use my WordPress templates on justaddtutor.com . They're based on the design principles and copywriting tactics that I've learned through exhaustive trial and error can convert visitors into clients. You might find prettier tutoring website templates, but you won't find any that are more effective.

Finding a place to do your tutoring

The place you do your tutoring is not the most important decision you make. As long as it's quiet, professional, in a reasonable location, and has free, fast Internet, you'll be okay.
However, if you ever want to charge a respectable amount of money per hour ($100 or more), I'd highly recommend that you join a coworking space. The coworking space I'm at, WeWork, is centrally located near public transportation (important for Boston), has free coffee and fruit-infused water, and provides me with a business address. Plus, it has a great, professional interior design.

WeWork only costs me $350/month. As an investment in my credibility, it's worth it. People are more willing to pay you if you appear professional (which they read as trustworthy). A coworking space is great for that.

WeWork has opened up offices pretty much everywhere. If you live in a city, there's probably one near you. If you want to schedule a tour of a nearby

WeWork, and tip me some extra money (at no charge to yourself), then follow this link.

Regardless of where you choose to work, once you do find a location, put it on your website, Google My Business, and Yelp accounts. First of all, this will make you more trustworthy. Second of all, Internet searches that rely on location (like "tutors near me") will use your location to provide information to potential clients.

Setting prices and getting money for your tutoring services

Pricing is a complicated subject. Tutoring is a nebulous service with no qualifications necessary, so tutoring can cost anywhere from $10/hr to $1000/hr (seriously, I've known people who charge that much). In short, nobody knows what tutoring is supposed to cost.

Here's what I'd say, then, about pricing. First of all, you need to figure out what your niches are. There's no way you can tutor every subject, so get specific ("Algebra II" rather than "high school math"). Once your niches are established, do research on what other people are charging online and on sites like

Wyzant and University Tutor. Then charge more than 75% of them.

The idea here is to position yourself as a premium service. Nobody knows what tutoring is supposed to cost, so people will judge your services by your pricing. In fact, one of the strange things you'll find (and that I found) is that the number of people who hire me has very little to do with the amount I charge. I have raised prices a few times, and I've never had a drop in clientele.

GMAT Tutoring Rates — $160/hr for the harder exam

$1600 for 10 hours

$1100 for 5 hours

$250 for 1 hour

(Note: discounts are available depending on financial need and individual circumstance. Contact me for more information.)

LSAT and GRE Tutoring Rates — $100/hr

$1000 for 10 hours

$625 for 5 hours

$150 for 1 hour

(Note: discounts are available depending on financial need and individual circumstance. Contact me for more information.)

Consulting Rates

$300 for 1 week

$1100 for 1 month

I charge more for GMAT because it's harder, and because GMAT takers are thinking about business school. A good business school is a great investment financially, so people feel okay about paying more for a good tutor.

When you sell these services to clients, sell them as hourly packages with a minimum number of hours required. Unless people are absolutely insistent, I never work less than 10 hours with someone. If people want to work less than 10 hours with me, I increase my hourly rate.

Tell people that you'll provide unlimited email support as long as you are meeting with them consistently. Only some of my clients take advantage of this, but everyone's always happy to hear it. I used to not include that caveat (meeting with them consistently), but then I had trouble with some people who'd use my email support continuously but never show up for tutoring sessions.

Always require people to pay upfront. It is so unpleasant to chase after money that people owe you. It always feels like you're about to burn a bridge with them, and in fact I have burned bridges doing so before. It's much easier if you just set a firm line: no money, no work. That way, if people enjoy working with you, they will continue to pay you in order to get the right to work with you. I ask for 5 or 10 hours payment before we meet (so, if we meet for 10 hours, I ask for 5 hours' payment before the first hour, then 5 hours' payment after the fourth).

Practically speaking, I use Venmo or Paypal for money from people. In doing so, I am actually doing something risky, as Paypal (which owns both services) has been known to freeze money in people's account for little to no reason. They are not a bank, and can freeze money if they want to. I deal with this risk by always transferring out money to my bank account as soon as I receive it, and keeping watch on my bank account to make sure the money transfers in. *Never keep a large balance in your Paypal or Venmo account.*

Dress code for tutoring

Honestly, this is non-existent. I briefly went through a period where I dressed nicely when I met with people. Then I gave up. Now I just wear clean t-shirts and clean jeans, and I'm much happier. As long as you don't look like a bum, you'll be fine.

Dealing with difficult clients as a tutor

As an independent tutor, you will come across people who think they can push you around. Even the nicest person can turn into a jerk if their rent is due and bank account is empty. Here's how you deal with these people.

First thing, an ounce of prevention is worth a pound of cure. If someone is being overly difficult or irrational during the sales process (negotiating immediately on price, or being habitually late to meetings), then they will likely be a bad client. You should not work with them unless you absolutely need the money. If you do work with them, be prepared to keep a tight leash on them.

Second, payment in advance solves a lot of issues. You won't have to wait for money, and if you ever need to charge them for something, you can simply email them, "Hey, I've charged you an hour's worth of my time. You now have 4 hours remaining of the 5 hours you paid for."

I employ this tactic a lot with people who are late. If they're late, I will still end at the agreed-upon time, and charge them as if we met the whole time. After all, I gave the time to use how they pleased. If they want to use 30 minutes of that time by me waiting for them to arrive, that's their prerogative.

With missing classes, I charge for the whole time if there's no notice. If there's less than 24 hours notice, I let it slide once, but warn them by email and say, "Hi, next time could you tell me in advance? Late notice plays havoc on my schedule." If they're late again, I charge them.

I pull a similar tactic with more than 24 hours notice cancellations if I feel like my clients are taking advantage of my good nature. I send them a warning, first, then I charge them if they do it again. Fortunately, it's rare that I actually have to charge people.

One thing that's important to know is that charging people cancellation fees is a bit of an unfriendly move. When you do it, try to be very apologetic, so as to get them on board as much as possible: "I'm really sorry, but I'm going to have to charge you for the lesson you missed. As I said, it gives me a lot of trouble when people frequently cancel, as it's hard enough to fit in every student's lessons as it is. I hope you understand, and I apologize again."

Taxes and deductions for tutoring

Taxes seem very frightening to most people. However, you can rest assured that they are actually not that bad.

As a tutor, you are probably going to be a sole proprietor, assuming you have no plans for taking on debt or employees. So, for tax purposes, you're just going to use your Social Security Number. If you want to hire employees or take out a loan, talk to an accountant.

When it comes time to pay your taxes, you can just use TaxAct. TaxAct is like TurboTax, and it allows you to file your taxes online. When you file your taxes, you are going to report your income and expenses on a form called Schedule 1040. This will be very straightforward. TaxAct is free if you make under $53,000 a year.

Income is everything you earned from your business (tutoring payments and peripheral products). Expenses are everything you spent directly on your business: supplies, testing fees, advertising, and office rent. Don't deduct things as expenses that weren't directly for your business. Report all the income you made. That's pretty much it. Also, if you're worried about being audited, don't be! An incredibly small fraction of people get audited.

The only reasons people get audited are:

1. They report nonsense, like a business that has made zero income 5 years in a row.
2. They report something that goes directly against a form, like if you don't report income that someone else claimed they paid you through a form 990.

3. They report something that is an IRS trigger point, like a home office deduction (the IRS hates those).
4. The IRS gets a tip. Seriously, their single biggest way of busting tax evasion is by disgruntled ex-employees and ex-wives. They take tips super seriously.

So don't worry about being audited!

However, you should worry about saving money up for taxes. Because you're not getting paid as an employee, you will have to pay taxes yourself. You need to pay taxes 4 times per year. Assume that roughly ⅓ of the money you earn is going to be taken by the IRS (yeah, it really sucks). So put ⅓ of the money you earn aside.

You will be paying 7.5% more in taxes as a self-employed person than you were as an employed person, thanks to the self-employment tax. If you don't like it, write your representative. Seriously, please do, because I hate it as well.

Bookkeeping

I find bookkeeping for tutoring super easy. My income is tracked through my Venmo, Paypal, and occasional checks. When it comes time to pay taxes, I just import my Venmo, Paypal, and bank account into Google Sheets, remove the non-tutoring related income, and that's it.

My expenses are paid through a single credit card, my Citicard DoubleCash (2% on all purchases!). When it comes time to pay taxes, I just import the expenses from that into Google Sheets and sort for my known expenses (pretty much just advertising and office rent, at this point).

Beyond that, all of my tutoring clients pay in blocks of 5 or 10 hours, so I just keep track of their hours on my Google Calendar along with when I'm supposed to be meeting them. When 5 hours is up, I can usually remember if they paid in a block of 5 or 10 hours. If I can't, I just check my email.

Fri Oct 20, 2017	10 - 11am	Meet with Chris hours 1 and 2
Fri Oct 27, 2017	10 - 11am	Meet with Chris hours 3 and 4
Fri Nov 10, 2017	10 - 11am	Meet with Chris hours 5 and 6

Again, it's very straightforward. Everything I use records itself. Also, when you sell services, there's never any input costs, so you never have to worry about that either. Once you have your advertising and office rent settled, those costs are pretty fixed as well, so there's no need to worry.

How to Teach as a Tutor

Executive Summary: Generally speaking, a teacher should be enthusiastic, optimistic, and able to make their students embrace failure. The best techniques are to organize explicitly, be repetitive, and be ready to vary levels of guidedness for the student. I'm a big fan of using [an error log](#) as an organizational and motivational tool.

One of the downsides of being independent is that, sadly enough, most of my worries and mental energy aren't actually about teaching. I'm so concerned about getting new clients and keeping them that I find it hard to devote enough time to serving my current clients as best as I can.

I suspect the same is true of most tutors and teachers. There's so much other stuff to worry about that it's hard to get time to perfect the craft.

Fortunately, I've gotten enough of my other concerns on autopilot right now that I have had some time to codify and perfect the way that I teach through experimentation and analysis.

Here's what I've found is the best way for tutors to teach.

Optimal teaching strategy for tutors
General thoughts about teaching

First of all, your job is to transmit information from your brain to your client's. You are doing this for the purpose of achieving their specific goa (in my case, getting their target score on their chosen test). Therefore, make sure that the information you transmit is useful, and that it's not useless. You should be focusing on, reiterating, and explaining useful information. If you spend a long time on personal anecdotes or irrelevant asides, that is what your students will remember from their lesson. That is bad.

Also, most learning processes are unpleasant. Very few people enjoy doing GRE or GMAT problems. To combat this, people need to view studying as a sprint, rather than as a stroll. They need to immerse themselves in the material for a couple hours a day. Much like literal immersion in cold water, it is easier to just embrace the unpleasantness and tackle it head-on, rather than dipping their toe in but never engaging. Part of the reason I meet with people for 2 hours a week is to encourage this sort of immersion.

Immersion makes it less likely that they'll quit in the middle of learning. Your clients will see improvements regularly, they'll remember what they've been learning, and they'll be forced to change their lifestyle to accommodate their learning. Much like how small commitments in the sales process makes your clients more likely to follow through, adjusting their lifestyle makes your clients more likely to keep with the learning process.

Finally, a teacher's job is to be an enthusiastic optimist. If what you teach is difficult (and if people are hiring you, it almost certainly is), at some point your clients will become bored, annoyed, frustrated, or some combination of the three. That is natural, and not a slight on you or your teaching ability.

When your students express their displeasure with the learning process, you need to acknowledge that their complaints are valid, but then deflect them with optimism. They should think that you heard them, but that you believe in their abilities.

For instance, if your student messes up the same thing for the thousandth time, and says, "I suck!" You should respond, "Yeah, you're having a bit of a tough time right now. But, you gotta get things wrong before you get them right."

If you are a pessimist, your student will be a pessimist a thousand times over. They are taking guidance from you on how to feel. Then they become unhappy, discouraged, and quit. Don't let that happen!

Specific recommendations for effective tutoring

So now for my specific recommendations, which are long and a bit cumbersome. For the purposes of this section, I'm going to use the extended example of giving the lessons on my website as a several day seminar. It seems pleasantly meta, and I assume you're pretty much an expert in this stuff by now.

Create a learning structure
Explicit hierarchical structure and progress tracking

For any big subject, students need to have a mental model of what the overall field looks like, and how what they're learning right now fits into the big picture. So, for example, if I was teaching the lessons on this website as a seminar, I'd start off with a broad overview of my business strategy: web presence, advertising, sales process, working with the student. Then I'd drill down into a specific topic, like the web page in web presence, then go further into the importance of proof, social proof, and credentials in creating a good web page.

Here's a visual example of what I mean.

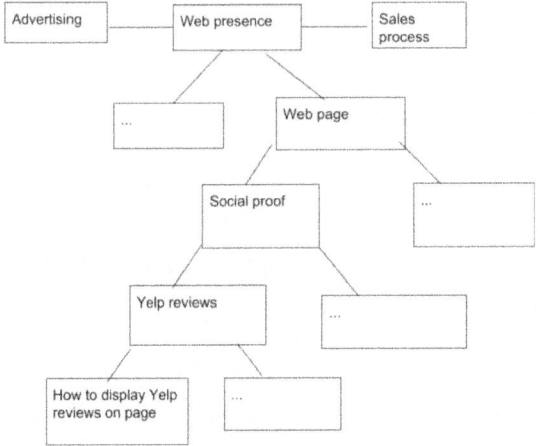

An explicitly hierarchical learning structure. There's no doubt to the student about what they're learning now, what they're learning next, or the purpose of what they're learning in the broader knowledge scheme they're supposed to know.

In the seminar, this structure would be referred to explicitly and repeatedly. Every student would understand why they are learning a certain aspect of my business strategy (like how to display social proof for your web page), and what its its purpose is in my overall business strategy. To the greatest extent possible, students would never be confused about how to execute a piece of my business philosophy or, even worse, be unfamiliar with my philosophy entirely.

This explicit structure also allows for progress tracking. Students would be familiar with all the aspects of my business strategy (e.g. peripheral products, blog posts, etc.). Being familiar with all the aspects of the strategy is a crucial step towards mastering the strategy as a whole. Progress tracking is: a motivational tool for students, as they can see what they've learned and feel happy about it; an analytical tool for students, as the weaknesses or holes in their understanding are apparent (like if they've never really understood sales calls); and a planning tool for students, as they can see what they will learn next.

In my own tutoring, I use an error log for progress tracking. I've given an example of one below. Notice how the error log is set-up with explicit mentions of type of questions, so students can plan out what they will cover; difficulty, so they can measure their expertise; and color-coding, so they can immediately visually see where they need improvement.

	Problem Solving	Link	Difficulty	Percentile	Type	First attempt	Second attempt	Third attempt	Fourth attempt
2	1	http://gmatclub.c	Easy	45%	Arithmetic: Percents				
3	2	http://gmatclub.c	Easy	5%	Arithmetic: Operations w				
4	3	https://gmatclub.	Easy	5%	Arithmetic: Ratio and pro				
5	4	http://gmatclub.c	Easy	15%	Arithmetic: Operations w				
6	5	https://gmatclub.	Easy	55%	Arithmetic: Applied probl				
7	6	https://gmatclub.	Easy	45%	Arithmetic: Percents				
8	7	http://gmatclub.c	Easy	65%	Algebra: Applied problem				
9	8	http://gmatclub.c	Easy	45%	Arithmetic: Operations w				
10	9	http://gmatclub.c	Easy	3%	Algebra: Simplifying alge				
11	10	http://gmatclub.c	Easy	75%	Arithmetic: Percents				
12	11	http://gmatclub.c	Medium	95%	Arithmetic: Probability				
13	12	http://gmatclub.c	Easy	15%	Algebra: First-degree equ	Took too long			
14	13	http://gmatclub.c	Easy	45%	Algebra: First-degree equ				
15	14	http://gmatclub.c	Easy	45%	Arithmetic: Statistics	4/10			
16	15	http://gmatclub.c	Easy	65%	Arithmetic: Percents	4/10			
17	16	https://gmatclub.	Easy	65%	Algebra: Inequalities	4/10			

Ideally, all of the color coded cells would be dated, so the student would know when they last got a question wrong or right. This lets them return to the question periodically, and get the solution into their long-term memory.

Goals (short, intermediate, long)

Anything that's difficult to learn will have problem with attrition. This problem is magnified if there's not a clear sense of structure to the learning. While that's somewhat addressed in 1, it's also important to have clear, universal goals set by the instructor. These goals need to be universal in the sense of "here's what any person should learn in sequence".

In our hypothetical seminar, I'd make these goals as explicit as sections on my website. They don't need to be super specific, as in "know how to retarget by the end of the second day of the seminar". They can be general, like "get comfortable with the ins and outs of Google's advertising option by the end of the second day". But the goals do need to be explicit, and there needs to be doubts or ambiguity about their content or when students should tackle them.

If it's not feasible for the instructor to state the goals in the seminar for whatever reason, the goals would be written, displayed, and made known among every student. Every student would be able to immediately answer two questions: what they've learned, and what they should learn next. This prevents them from being overwhelmed.

No student should be made to feel discouraged or ashamed about being slow to progress in sequence. People have different skills and motivation, and progressing slowly (or even regressing in extreme circumstances) is better than quitting. However, going to a multi-day seminar and not knowing what to focus on is not a good thing.

In my own tutoring, I set up these goals by coming up with strategies for individual sections, and giving students ways to measure how well they're implementing the strategy. Implementing these strategies successfully on homework is a short-term goal, on practice tests are intermediate goals, and on their live exam is a long-term goal. It is fine if students are slow to implement my strategies and achieve improvement on practice tests. As long as they continue to achieve the next goal in front of them (like learning how to implement my strategies on the next homework question), they will eventually get there.

Improving the in-class experience
Repetition/callback

Along with structure and goals, repetition is a key part of learning. Each lesson should be structured in the beginning as "This is what we are going to learn". In the middle: "this is what we are learning". In the end: "this is what we have learned".

From an instructor's perspective, the repetition seems unnecessary and boring. But that is because the instructor doesn't have to get over the shock of unfamiliarity. To a student, the concepts and tools I use in my tutoring are like the words of a new language. Even after hearing them, it's very difficult to use them.

Repetition also helps orient the students as to where they are in the structure. If students understand the concepts well enough to tune out the instructor's repetition, then they are able to think more deeply about the concept, and situate it logically.

This repetition includes repeating over a period of days. Calling back to earlier lessons helps students understand deeper, and is both satisfying and allows for a deeper understanding of the concept learned previously and the concept being learned currently.

This is, in fact, how you're using this book right now, or at least I hope you are. You read something, read it again, take some notes, then maybe go back to another section to compare what I said before. The repetition improves your understanding, as does the reference to what was said earlier.

In my tutoring, if students struggle with a question, I approach it with this repetition in mind. I tell them how I'd set it up. Then I set it up, and walk them through my approach. Finally, I remind them how I set it up and approached it. Often, I then ask my students to try the approach on another, similar question, cementing the repetition.

Takeaways from lesson

Even if a lesson is well taught in the moment, it is too easy to forget it as soon as a student goes home and the distractions of everyday life come roaring back. Takeaways from the lesson give something for students to hold onto once the lesson is over.

If you want to give someone a takeaway to remember, keep it to a sentence or two. The idea isn't to give the student all the details you gave in the seminar, but instead to give them a trigger for recalling. If you want to give them all the details, provide it in video or document format. Once they remember their trigger, they can use the video or document to remember the details (see. "Supplementary Material" for more information).

Often, I have a key phrase that I use with certain sorts of problems while tutoring. For example, faced with a logic problem, I ask the students: "What's the author's conclusion?" This begins the sequence that I use to solve logic problems. When the student works on their own, they can remember this trigger to start the sequence.

During lessons, vary levels of guidedness

During a lesson, it's up to the teacher how best to teach a concept, technique, or tool. If it's something that's very technical and being taught for the first time, the teacher should be precise and detail exactly how it works step-by-step. If it's more of a concept or feeling, the teacher should give goals, and the student should do work on their own (thinking, writing, etc.) according to the teacher's goals or guidelines. If the teacher is testing something that's already been learned, the student should be able to answer without any guidelines from the teacher.

Many teachers have trouble with intermediate levels of guidedness. When they teach something new, they want to dictate exactly what the student should do. When they let the students do it on their own, they give them zero guidance. However, this is a very hard gap for a student to bridge on their own. There's a big difference between seeing someone do something (or being told to act in a certain way), and doing it yourself, especially in a new or unfamiliar situation.

To give a concrete example, when first teaching my sales process in a seminar, I would demonstrate exactly how I'd guide the conversation, and give step by step explanations of what I'm doing. Then, I'd ask students to break out and try it on their own. At that point, I would repeat the step by step instructions as the students copy what I did. Once the students are comfortable with that, I'd give the students broad, general steps, and ask them to progress through the sales conversation themselves. Finally, I'd ask the students to carry out the entire sales conversation from start-to-finish without any input from me.

In my tutoring, I first teach techniques by performing the technique on a question myself, narrating my thought process as I do so and taking clear notes. I then key the student through the techniques on another problem, asking leading questions to get them to perform the right processes. My next step is to ask open-ended questions on yet another problem, asking the student what the steps in the process should be. Finally, I let them perform the technique on another problem on their own.

The idea here is to reduce the cognitive load of the students. Remembering how the conversation is supposed to go and performing it correctly is hard. Transition from being instructed to doing it on a student's own needs to be gradual. Otherwise, what ends up happening is that students don't quite remember correctly, then proceed to practice incorrectly. This either results in them not remembering what's taught, or, even worse, remembering it incorrectly, giving them problems down the road.

Give your students a chance to fail in controlled ways

Going along with teacher guidedness is the idea of giving students a chance to fail. This might either sound ridiculous or obvious, depending on your view of teaching, but first I need to clarify what I mean by this. Failure is when you try, and your try obviously doesn't work.

So, misremembering a concept and being corrected is a failure. Setting up a tool incorrectly so that it clearly doesn't work is a failure. Having a customer not convert after a sales conversation is not usually a failure, because it's normally unclear where your error was, or what you should have done to correct it.

As you might imagine, much like guidedness, failures lie on a spectrum from 100% teacher controlled (like misremembering a concept when asked) to 0% teacher controlled (like failing to remember how to correctly set up tools for your own website). The intermediate levels of teacher-controlled failure (like saying something wrong when role-playing a sales conversation) are likewise lacking in most education.

Failure should be regular in any class. If students do not fail, they will not learn. And so any class must be a place where failure is welcomed and encouraged. This is difficult for students, because failure is not as fun as succeeding. The instructor must strive to create an atmosphere where students are, if not happy to fail, then not unhappy to fail.

Improvements in Communication
Narrative

During class itself, the easiest way to teach is by a narrative structure. Not in the sense of creating a complex story, but in the sense of creating clear reasons why we are doing certain things in a certain way. This allows for deeper understanding of the concepts being taught, and aids with retention.

For example, when teaching the idea of writing blog posts that people search for on Google, the teacher could explain that the entrepreneur *wants* to anticipate what people search for and provide answers for it. It's a simple wording change from simply "anticipate what people search for and provide answers for it", but it transforms the idea from a static instruction to a dynamic one, in which entrepreneurs are thinking, adjusting, and evolving in their goal to anticipate searches. Furthermore, it leads the student to useful questions: "why should I anticipate what people search for?" "How do I anticipate what people search for?" "How will Google know that I'm providing good answers?"

These can be answered by the instructor. Of course, the instructor can share these details without the questions being asked, but it's easier for the student to remember and understand an answer when the student is motivated to know the answer. People like motivations.

In my tutoring, I phrase techniques in a similar manner. On the GMAT, there is a question type which asks what information you'd need to make a math problem solvable. Instead of saying "knowing the precise value of x makes the equation solvable", I phrase it as: "I need to know the value of x if I want to solve this. How can I find the value of x?"

It's the same idea, worded differently. People respond to narratives in a way that they don't respond to abstract concepts. That's why I have been illustrating these examples with a hypothetical narrative.

Compliment liberally, criticize gently

One of the easiest ways to motivate a student, create a welcoming learning environment, and just make people like learning is to compliment them. Compliments are key to a healthy learning environment, but it is amazing how seldom teachers use them.

For example, in my hypothetical seminar, I imagine I'd have a huge problem in keeping around people who are technophobic. People who are already uncomfortable operating new pieces of software could become easily discouraged once they realize the range of new interfaces I'd ask them to work with. Being overwhelmed leads to fear, and then soon after that the attitude that "this just isn't something for someone like me".

Compliments help keep people around, and working on what the teacher thinks is appropriate. Criticisms are also useful (like for letting people know they've failed), but they're dangerous when used casually. It's easy to discourage or anger people with criticisms, which leads to unproductive learning environments. Criticisms should be obvious but gentle. So, if someone does something incorrectly, the teacher can say, "Not quite. Try doing this." It's obvious that it's a criticism, and that the student failed, but it's not framed in a discouraging manner.

In my tutoring, I do the same thing. I am always complimentary when people get questions correct, and gentle to tell people when they get a question wrong. When people ask me if I'm frustrated at their slow progress, I always assure them that I am happy to help them and happy to see them trying. The tutor sets the mood, and their words carry a lot of weight. Tests are a source of great anxiety to people, and it is a tutor's job to alleviate that anxiety.

After Class
Supplementary material and long term memory retention

It's easy for a teacher to fall into the trap of thinking that, if they point students towards supplementary material, the students will stop taking the teacher seriously, or even stop coming altogether. This is far from the case. The enemies of teaching are forgetfulness and apathy. Students will very rarely quit going to classes because they learn too much. Far more often, they will quit because they forget too much, and they don't want to put in the effort to remember again.

So supplementary material is crucial. There are many videos, books, and webpages available online, but most students will not seek these out on their own. They need explicit instruction to seek them out, and they need to be tested on the material. This testing should, of course, be friendly. As before, failure must be a welcome part of the learning environment.

Supplementary material is perhaps the only way that students can assist their long term memory and their progress tracking. If a tool or concept is used regularly, it remains in short term memory, and is easily recalled. But, if it is not used regularly, then it is unlikely a student will remember it again months later, unless they have been reviewing it through supplementary material.

For my tutoring, I make peripheral products that I provide to my tutoring clients for free. I also point them towards high-quality, free online resources. Again, my worry is never losing clients to these online resources. My worry is losing clients when they give up on the test. This prevents that.

Conclusion and Standing Offer

You finished the book. Congrats!

Now, here's the single most important thing to take away from this book: **you need to act to start or improve your tutoring business!**

Don't just read this book and forget about it. If you can't take action at this present moment, then put <u>specific events in your calendar</u> to implement these steps.

There is no easy path to building a strong tutoring business, but there is a clear path. I've presented it here.

Oh, by the way, here's my Standing Offer:

If you want to talk to me about tutoring, education, or striking out on your own, I am more than happy to talk to you. No matter who you are or what your current background is, shoot me an email and I will respond.

My email is info@justaddtutor.com, and my name is Trevor Klee (I suppose I forgot to introduce myself, sorry). I will be really happy if you send me emails about any of these topics:

1. Asking for advice on tutoring, education, entrepreneurship, or just generally striking out on your own

2. Asking for collaboration on a project

3. An article you've written that you think I should read

4. An article you've read that you think I should read

If I do not respond to you immediately, it's probably because I'm busy. It is not because I was not happy to receive your email. If it's been a week, and I still haven't responded to you, send a follow-up! I sometimes lose track of emails.

Best of luck with your tutoring business!

CPSIA information can be obtained
at www.ICGtesting.com
Printed in the USA
LVHW111223020620
657221LV00002B/444